# The Secret Adversary (Illustrated)

–

## Agatha Christie

–

**Adapted for kids aged 9-11 Grades 4-7, Key Stages 2 and 3 US-English Edition Large Print**

**by Lazlo Ferran**

GW00750550

PRINTING HISTORY

First Edition

Copyright © 2018 by Lazlo Ferran

Published by Future City Publishing, London.

Printed in 11 point Times New Roman

*Classics adapted by Lazlo Ferran:*

The Mysterious Affair at Styles – Adapted For Kids
The Mysterious Affair at Styles – Adapted For Kids – Large Print
The Mysterious Affair at Styles – Kids Colouring Book
The Mysterious Affair at Styles – Kids Fun Exercise Book
The Mysterious Affair at Styles – For EFL/ESL Level B2 Students
The Mysterious Affair at Styles – Vocabulary Stretcher
The Secret Adversary – Adapted For Kids (US and UK Editions)
The Secret Adversary – For Kids (US and UK Editions) – Large Print
The Secret Adversary – Kids Colouring Book
The Secret Adversary – Kids Fun Exercise Book
The Secret Adversary – For EFL/ESL Level B2 Students (US and UK Editions)
The Secret Adversary – Vocabulary Stretcher (US and UK Editions)
Frankenstein – Adapted For Kids
Frankenstein – Adapted For Kids – Large Print
Frankenstein – Kids Colouring Book
Frankenstein – Kids Fun Exercise Book
Frankenstein – For EFL/ESL Level B2 Students
Frankenstein – Vocabulary Stretcher
MacBeth – Adapted For Kids
MacBeth – Kids Colouring Book
MacBeth – Kids Fun Exercise Book
MacBeth – Adapted For Kids – Large Print
MacBeth – For EFL/ESL Level B2 Students
MacBeth – Vocabulary Stretcher

*Other books by Lazlo Ferran:*

Ordo Lupus and the Temple Gate
Too Bright the Sun
The Hole Inside the Earth

# Contents

# Prologue

It was 2 p.m. on the afternoon of May 7, 1915, during the First World War. The ocean liner Lusitania had been struck by two German torpedoes and was sinking rapidly, while the boats were being launched quickly. The women and children were being lined up to wait their turn. Some still clung desperately to husbands and fathers; others clutched their children closely to their chests. One girl stood alone. She was not more than eighteen. She did not seem afraid, and her serious, steady eyes looked straight ahead.

"I beg your pardon."

A man's voice beside her startled her and made her turn. She had noticed the speaker more than once amongst the first–class passengers. There had been a hint of mystery about him that had appealed to her. He spoke to no one. If anyone spoke to him, he was quick to turn them away. Also, he had a nervous way of looking over his shoulder with a swift, suspicious glance.

She noticed now that he was very upset. There were beads of sweat on his brow. He was obviously in a state of fear. And yet he did not strike her as the kind of man who would be afraid to meet death!

"Yes?" Her grave eyes met his.

He stood looking at her with a kind of desperate hesitation.

"It must be!" he muttered to himself. "Yes—it's the only way." Then aloud he said abruptly:

"You are an American?"

"Yes."

"A patriotic one?"

The girl blushed.

"I guess you've no right to ask such a thing! Of course I am!"

"Don't be upset. You wouldn't be if you knew how much there was at stake. But I've got to trust some one—and it must be a woman."

"Why?"

"Because women and children will go into the lifeboats first." He looked round and lowered his voice. "I'm carrying papers—top-secret papers. They may make all the difference to the British and Americans in the war. You understand? These papers have *got* to be saved! They have more chance with you than with me. Will you take them?"

The girl held out her hand.

"Wait—I must warn you. There may be a risk—if I've been followed. I don't think I have, but one never knows. If so, there will be danger. Have you the nerve to go through with it?"

The girl smiled. "I'll go through with it all right. And I'm real proud to be chosen! What am I to do with them afterwards?"

"Watch the newspapers! I'll advertise in the personal column of the Times, beginning 'Shipmate.' At the end of three days if there's nothing—well, you'll know I'm dead. Then take the packet to the American Embassy and deliver it into the Ambassador's own hands. Is that clear?"

"Quite clear."

"Then be ready—I'm going to say good–bye." He took her hand in his. "Good–bye. Good luck to you," he said in a louder tone.

Her hand closed on the waterproof packet that he had held in his palm.

The Lusitania settled with a more obvious lean to the right. In answer to a quick command, the girl went forward to take her place in the boat.

# Chapter 1 — The Young Adventurers Ltd.

Tom, always called Tommy, and Prudence, called Tuppence by all her friends, had known each other since they were children but had last met when Tommy had been wounded in World War One and sent to recover in the hospital where Tuppence had been working. Tuppence bumped into Tommy outside Piccadilly London Underground station, so they went for a cup of tea in a small, but busy, café.

Tommy sat down opposite her. His bared head revealed a shock of carefully slicked–back red hair. His face was pleasantly ugly—plain, yet the face of a gentleman and sportsman. His brown suit was well cut but dangerously near the end of its life.

They were a very modern–looking couple as they sat there. Tuppence had no claim to beauty, but there was character and charm in the elf-like lines of her little face, with its determined chin and large, wide–apart grey eyes that looked mistily out from under straight, black brows. She wore a small, bright green hat over her black, bobbed hair, and her extremely short and rather shabby skirt revealed a pair of unusually pretty ankles. Her appearance made a brave attempt at smartness.

"I can't order more than tea!" Tommy said. "I'm broke!"

"Me too! After more than six months in that hospital they eventually promoted me to Wardmaid, complete with bucket and brush. Since then Prudence Cowley, fifth daughter of Archdeacon Cowley, has driven a delivery truck, a long-distance truck and a general's staff car. But now I can't find anything, even though I have applied for loads!"

"Me neither! After being brought back to good health by the smiles of Tuppence Cowley, Lieutenant Thomas Beresford was sent by the British Army to Turkey and then Egypt. There I remained until the end of the War! I thought it would be easy to get a job when I came back, but nobody seems to want a soldier. I won't have a cent by the end of this week."

"I will have to go home to mum and dad if I don't find something! No rich relatives?"

"My uncle. But he hates me."

"Oh."

Tuppence's large, grey eyes misted over. "Never mind. It's so good to see you!"

Tommy and Tuppence had always shared the same sense of humour, so it didn't take long for him to lean close to her and whisper:

"Funny chat one hears. Two guys passed me in the street today, talking about Jane Finn. Such an unusual name! Jane; so English. Finn; so Irish!"

They were interrupted by the waiter bringing their cups of tea, but conversation soon returned to the dreaded subject of cash.

"Money! Money! Money!" Tuppence burst out. "That's all I can think about! I'm desperate. I've tried to think of everything. I'm even thinking of marrying a rich man."

"Oh Tuppence! You can't!"

"Why not? A lot of girls do. And you can marry a rich woman!"

"I don't think so. I'm not good-looking enough."

"Oh, what are we to do? We've tried all the usual ways of earning money. Tommy! Let's try the unusual ways! Let's be adventurers!"

"Okay! How do we begin?"

"That's the difficulty. If we could advertise, people might hire us to commit crimes for them."

"Great career for a priest's daughter!"

"Oh, but the moral guilt wouldn't be ours. We would just be doing the crime *for* somebody! Let's call it the Young Adventurers Ltd. Now, we need to advertise. Got a pencil? Guys always seem to have one."

"Here you go."

Tuppence grabbed a napkin and wrote:

> Two young adventurers for hire. Willing to do anything, go any-where. Pay must be good. No rea-sonable offer refused.

"Wouldn't unreasonable be more accurate?" Tommy said.

"Oh Tommy! You're a genius!"

Tuppence added 'un' to the beginning of 'reasonable' and looked proudly at her advert. She handed the napkin over to Tommy and said:

"Times, I think. Reply to Box so-and-so. I expect it will be about thirty cents. Here's fifteen for my share."

Tommy's face burned red. He stared at the napkin and then grinned.

"Shall we do it Tuppence? Really?"

"Let's drink to it!"

Tuppence held out her cup, containing the last dregs of tea, and Tommy toasted their advert by tapping his cup against hers. They finished the tea, and then Tuppence stood up.

"We should meet tomorrow," Tommy said. "Where?"

"Twelve o'clock. Piccadilly Tube station."

Tuppence walked home to save money, but a man stopped her in half way across St. James's Park.

"Excuse me. May I speak to you for a moment?"

# Chapter 2 — Mr. Whittington's Offer

Tuppence turned sharply, intending to refuse the man, but his smart appearance made her hesitate. Reading her thoughts, the man said quickly:

"I mean no disrespect. I have a proposal for you."

Tuppence looked him up and down. He was a big man, clean shaven, with a heavy jawline. His eyes were small and cunning and shifted their glance under her direct gaze.

"Well?"

"I overheard part of your conversation in the café."

"And?"

"I think I may be of use to you."

"You followed me?"

The man handed her a business card, which told her:

Mr. Edward Whittington, Estonia Glassware Co.

Below was an address.

"If you will call there at eleven o'clock tomorrow morning, I will lay out my proposal."

"Eleven o'clock? I'll be there."

He raised his hat with a flourish and walked away. Tuppence remained for some minutes gazing after him. Then she gave a curious movement of her shoulders, rather as a terrier dog shakes himself.

"The adventures have begun," she murmured to herself. "What does he want me to do, I wonder? There's something about you, Mr. Whittington, that I don't like at all. But, on the other hand, I'm not afraid of you. And as I've said before, and shall doubtless say again, little Tuppence can look after herself, thank you!"

A thrill filled Tuppence as she approached the building that contained the Estonia Glassware Co. just before eleven on the following morning. Tuppence knocked, and a middle-aged man let her in.

"I have an appointment with Mr. Whittington," Tuppence said.

"Will you come this way please," he replied, leading her to a door marked 'Private' and held it open to let her through.

Mr. Whittington sat behind a large desk covered with papers. Tuppence felt her feelings had been bright. There was something wrong about Mr. Whittington. The combination of his sleek suit and his shifty eye was not attractive.

"Please sit down," he said. "Let's get down to business. You are looking for work? Well, I have work for you. $100 now, and all expenses paid."

Tuppence eyed him warily.

"What kind of work?"

"A pleasant trip, that is all."

"Where to?"

"Paris."

"Oh!" said Tuppence thoughtfully. To herself she said: "Of course, if father heard that he would have a fit! But somehow I don't see Mr. Whittington in the role of the mad trickster."

"Yes," continued Whittington. "What could be nicer? Madame Colombier's in the Avenue de Neuilly. It's a lovely place."

Tuppence knew it was one of the best hotels in Paris.

"How long would I be there?" she asked.

"Oh, perhaps three months."

"That is all? No other conditions?"

"None. You would go as my young companion, but you can't communicate with any of your friends; this would have to be completely secret. You are English by the way?"

"Yes."

"But you have a slight American accent?"

"My best friend in the hospital where I worked was American. I probably picked it up from her. I can get rid of it."

"No! Actually, it will be easier if you act as an American. We won't have to explain your English background. Then—"

"Hm. How about my partner, Mr. Beresford? You saw us together yesterday?"

"Ah yes! I'm afraid we won't need his services."

"No deal then. It's either both of us or none."

"Oh, wait! Let me think."

Tuppence thought he would want a name, but she didn't want to use her own, so she said the first name that came into her head:

"Jane Finn."

Whittington's face turned purple with rage. He looked shocked as he hissed:

"So that's your game! Trying to trick me? Who blabbed? Rita?"

Tuppence wondered what had happened, but seeing Whittington looking scared made her wonder if she could exploit the situation. Without thinking she replied:

"No. Rita knows nothing about me."

"How much do you know?"

"Very little!"

Tuppence felt pleased when Whittington's anger increased. She had guessed correctly that boasting about knowing a lot would have made him suspicious.

"Stop teasing me! How much do you know? And how much do you want?"

"Suppose you pay a small deposit and we arrange another chat later?"

"Blackmail, eh?"

"No, payment for my services!" Tuppence replied, smiling sweetly.

Whittington grunted.

"You see, I am so very fond of money!" Tuppence added.

"Come in!" Whittington said, at a knock on the door.

The clerk came in and said:

"Telephone message for you, sir."

"That'll do, Brown."

The clerk withdrew and Whittington turned to Tuppence:

"Come tomorrow at the same time. I'm busy. Here's fifty to go on with."

He rapidly counted the bills and pushed them across the table. Tuppence carefully counted them, put them in her handbag and rose.

"Good morning, Mr. Whittington," she said, before leaving.

Tuppence sped lightly down the stairs. A wild happiness came over her. A hallway clock showed the time to be five minutes to twelve.

"Let's give Tommy a surprise!" murmured Tuppence, and hailed a cab.

The cab drew up outside Piccadilly Tube station. Tommy was just inside the entrance. His eyes opened wide as he hurried forward to help Tuppence out. She smiled at him, and said in a slightly posh voice: "Pay him, will you? I've got nothing smaller than a five–dollar bill!"

# Chapter 3 — A Setback

"I don't think the driver believed you!" Tommy said, after he had found enough change to pay the man.

"No," said Tuppence thoughtfully, "he didn't believe it. That's the strange part about speaking the truth. No one does believe it. I found that out this morning. Now let's go to lunch. How about the Savoy?"

"How about the Ritz?"

"On second thoughts, there's a good restaurant just around the corner. Come on!"

Tommy still thought Tuppence was joking about being rich, but when she ordered the most expensive items on the menu, he had to protest:

"We can't afford all that!"

"Can't we?"

Tuppence opened up her handbag to show Tommy the wad of money.

"Wow!" he cried. "We're rich! Where did you get all that? Did you steal from a bank?"

Tuppence told him everything.

"And the strange thing is," she concluded, "that I just made the name of Jane Finn up!"

"No, you didn't. I told you. Don't you re-member, I said yesterday I'd overheard two people talking about a female called Jane Finn?"

"Yes, you did! How amazing!" Tup-pence's voice trailed off. Suddenly she sat up straight.

"Tommy! What were they like, the two men?"

"One was a big guy, wearing a smart suit. Dark looks."

"That's him! Whittington! What was the other man like?"

"I can't remember. It was a weird name. I can't remember!"

"And people say freaky things don't hap-pen!"

Tuppence tucked into her desert, grin-ning.

"What's all this about?" Tommy asked.

"More money."

"Yes, that's all you can think about. But what will be your next step. You can't fool him for long."

"You're right. Here's the coffee. Let me think." After finishing her coffee, Tuppence said, "I know! I have a plan. It's simple. We just have to find out more."

"How?"

"You must follow Whittington tomorrow. Wait outside the building after I leave, but don't talk to me. Follow him when he comes out."

"Hm. Alright, it sounds like a plan."

But the following day Tuppence emerged from the building and walked straight up to Tommy.

"The office is empty!" she said. "He's gone. The whole company has gone!"

"That's the end of that then!"

"No, it's the beginning. Don't you see? If they are that scared of the name Jane Finn, there must be a lot involved. We'll be proper detectives and get to the bottom of it. Give me that pencil again."

Tommy read what she wrote:

WANTED: information on Jane Finn.

# Chapter 4 — Who Is Jane Finn?

The advert came out on Friday, so Tuppence and Tommy had agreed to meet that afternoon in the National Gallery of art. Tuppence sat on one of the red, velvet seats and stared at a J.M.W. Turner painting until Tommy arrived.

"Well?" Tuppence asked, hopefully.

"Which is your favourite painting?"

"Don't be cruel. Aren't there *any* answers?"

Tommy shook his head. "I didn't want to disappoint you. That's why I am late. The advert has appeared, and — there are only two answers!"

"Oh Tommy! You tease! Give them to me!"

Tuppence read the first reply out loud:

Dear Sir,
Referring to your advertisement in this morning's paper, I may be able to be of some use to you. Perhaps you could call and see me at the above address at eleven o'clock tomorrow morning.
Yours truly, A. Carter.

"27 Carshalton Gardens," said Tuppence, referring to the address. "That's Gloucester Road way. Plenty of time to get there if we tube."

Tuppence turned to the second letter and read that aloud too:

> Dear Sir,
> Re your advertisement, I would be glad if you would call round somewhere about lunchtime.
> Yours truly,
> Julius P. Hersheimmer. The Ritz

"Sounds German or perhaps a rich American," Tommy said.

"Now for Carter. Not much time. We'll have to take a cab."

Carshalton Terrace proved to be a line of very expensive, white houses. They knocked at number 27, and a maid answered the door. The house looked so respectable that Tuppence felt discouraged.

A tall man with a lean, hawk-like face and tired expression greeted and seated them in his study. There was something about him that made Tuppence feel less confident. He didn't seem to feel like beginning the discussion, so Tuppence said:

"We wanted to know—that is, would you be so kind as to tell us anything you know about Jane Finn?"

"Jane Finn? Ah!" Mr. Carter appeared to reflect. "Well, the question is, what do you know about her?"

"I don't see what that has to do with it!" Tuppence replied.

"Ah, but it has everything to do with it. What do you know?"

Tuppence crossed her arms and refused to reply, but Tommy suddenly said:

"I'll tell you what I know. I recognise you from France, sir. You were with the Secret Services. I knew you as—"

Mr. Carter held up his hand.

"No real names here. Mr. Carter will do. This is my cousin's house, by the way. She lets me borrow it when I need to."

"Fire away Tuppence!" Tommy said.

Tuppence told Mr. Carter everything, even about the Young Adventurers Ltd and their plans to make money.

"You're a strange couple," Mr. Carter said, when she had finished. "But you might succeed where others have failed. I believe in luck. Well, how about it? You're out for adventure. How would you like to work for me? All quite unofficial, you know. Expenses paid, and a modest amount of work?"

Tuppence gazed at him, her lips parted, her eyes growing wider and wider.

"What would we have to do?" she breathed.

"Just do what you're doing. Find Jane Finn."

"Yes, but—who *is* Jane Finn?"

Mr. Carter nodded gravely. "Yes, you're entitled to know that, I think." He leaned back in his chair, crossed his legs, brought the tips of his fingers together, and began the story in a low voice. He told them about the sinking of the Lusitania by a submarine, of a secret agent called Danvers, who had given a top-secret packet to Jane Finn, a passenger on the ship.

"Danvers drowned," Mr. Carter said. "His body washed up on the shore, but the packet was missing. Just before the ship sunk, he was seen talking to a young American girl. But we have tried to trace her and failed! Her name was Jane Finn, and she appeared on the passenger list, but she was an orphan and seems to have vanished. She came from a western state in America and had been offered a post in a Paris hospital. Why she didn't arrive we have no idea. We tracked her to Ireland, but beyond there— nothing!"

"What was in the parcel?" Tuppence asked.

"In 1915, at the height of the First World War, a secret agreement for peace was made between Germany and Great Britain. The agreement document was prepared by America, which was neutral at the time, but never signed. Of course, the War ended in a different way and the document was forgotten, but recently rumours spread that it still exists. That means that certain politicians could be connected with a document that would be considered shameful now. We fear that one of the socialist political parties might use it on Labour day to blackmail the government or worse, publish it and start a revolution."

"Wow!" Tommy said.

"Yes!" Mr. Carter continued. "We know the Russians are pouring gold into the country, hoping to start a revolution. We also know that a single man is organising it, a Mr. Brown, but we don't know his real identity. He runs an amazing organisation. His spies are everywhere. He always plays a minor role, acting as a clerk or servant."

"Oh!" Tuppence said, standing up. "I wonder? There was a clerk called Mr. Brown in Mr. Whittington's office."

Carter nodded.

"Probably him. What did he look like?"

"Well, I don't actually remember. He looked very ordinary. I don't remember anything unusual."

"Hm. People always say that. It's interesting that he always uses the name Brown. Perhaps it's the signature of a genius, in a way. Well, now you see what you're up against. I would hate something bad to happen to you. Are you sure you want the job?"

"I'll look after him!" Tuppence said, glancing at Tommy.

"And I'll look after her!" Tommy replied.

"Alright. Well, let me tell you that the revolutionaries have been threatening us with this document. The Government in England doesn't officially believe that they have it. I think they do, but they are missing something, and they are trying to find out more about Jane Finn from us!"

"What?" Tommy and Tuppence said, together.

"Yes, if I were them, I would get a girl to act as Jane Finn and take her to a Paris hotel, where she could meet people who might know something about Jane Finn in order to get information from them."

"Do you think that's what Whittington had in mind for me?" Tuppence asked.

"Don't you?"

# Chapter 5 — Mr. Julius P. Hersheimmer

Tuppence stood up to leave.

"Do you have any more information to help us?" Tommy asked.

"I think not. My own agents have failed, but you will come at it from a new angle, and that may allow you to succeed. But then again it may be harder now. I have a feeling time is now a factor. The Government is intending to crack down on the labour unions in the early part of next year, so this might be the time the uprising occurs."

"I think we had better be professional," Tuppence said. "How about funds?"

"Funds within reason, detailed at every point by you. But you can't refer back to us. If you are caught, we have nothing to do with you. You do understand?"

"Absolutely."

"Good. As for salary, shall we say at the rate of three hundred a year? And an equal sum for Mr. Beresford, of course."

"That's very generous!" Tuppence replied. "I am very good at bookkeeping, so I will keep proper accounts."

A few minutes later, Tommy and Tuppence were walking along Carshalton Terrace, their heads in a whirl.

"Tommy, who is Mr. Carter?"

He whispered in her ear, "The head of the Secret Services!"

"I like him. Pinch me Tommy! Ouch! Not that hard. Can you believe we're real secret agents now?"

"No! Let's go and have lunch."

But they both suddenly said together, "Julius P. Hersheimmer!"

"We'll just make it if we take a cab!" Tommy said, flagging one down.

They only just reached the Ritz hotel in time and were shown up to Mr. Hersheimmer's suite.

An impatient voice cried, "Come in," in answer to the page–boy's knock, and the lad stood aside to let them pass in. Mr. Julius P. Hersheimmer was a great deal younger than either Tommy or Tuppence had pictured him. The girl put him down as thirty–five. He was of middle height, but muscular and squarely built to match his jaw. His face was blunt but pleasant. No one could have mistaken him for anything but an American, though he spoke with very little accent.

"Get my note? Sit down and tell me right away all you know about my cousin."

"Your cousin?"

"Sure thing. Jane Finn." "Is she your cousin?" "My father and her mother were brother and sister," explained Mr. Hersheimmer carefully.

"Oh!" cried Tuppence. "Then you know where she is?"

"No!" Mr. Hersheimmer brought down his fist with a bang on the table. "I'm darned if I do! Don't you?"

"We advertised to receive information, not to give it," said Tuppence severely.

"I guess I know that. I can read. But I thought maybe it was her back history you were after, and that you'd know where she was now?"

"How do I know you haven't kidnapped her? Or that you will?"

"We haven't kidnapped your cousin. In fact, we're trying to find her. We're employed to do so."

Mr. Hersheimmer leant back in his chair. "Put me wise," he said sharply.

Tommy gave him a short version of the disappearance of Jane Finn, and of the possibility of her having been mixed up in "some political thing." He called Tuppence and himself private investigators hired to find her and added that they would be glad for any details.

Hersheimmer nodded.

"I guess it's all right. I was just a mite hasty. But London gets my goat! I only know little old New York. Just trot out your questions and I'll answer."

"When did you last see the dece—your cousin, I mean?" Tuppence asked.

"Never seen her," responded Mr. Hersheimmer.

"What?" demanded Tommy, astonished.

Hersheimmer turned to him.

"No, sir. As I said before, my father and her mother were brother and sister, just as you might be,"—Tommy did not correct this view of their relationship—"but they didn't always get on together. And when my aunt made up her mind to marry Amos Finn, who was a poor school teacher out West, my father was just mad! Said if he got rich, as he seemed about to do, she'd never see a cent of it. Well, the result was that Aunt Jane went out West and we never heard from her again."

"Go on!" Tommy said.

"Then he died—last fall—and I got the dollars. My conscious kept reminding me of Jane. Well, I figured it out that Amos Finn would never make money. He wasn't the sort. I hired a man to hunt her down. Result, she was dead, and Amos Finn was dead, but they'd left a daughter—Jane—who'd been torpedoed on the Lusitania on her way to Paris. She was saved, but nobody can find her! I'm off to Paris tomorrow to look there."

The energy of Mr. Hersheimmer was tremendous.

"But we can work together?" he added. "What about some lunch? Shall we have it up here, or go down to the restaurant?"

Oysters had just given place to fillet of sole when a card was brought to Hersheimmer.

"Inspector Japp, C.I.D. Scotland Yard again," he explained, when he sat down. "Another man this time. What does he expect I can tell him that I didn't tell the first chap? I hope they haven't lost that photograph. That Western photographer's place was burned down and all his negatives destroyed—this is the only copy in existence. I got it from the principal of the college there."

A terrible fear swept over Tuppence.

"You—you don't know the name of the man who came this morning?"

"Yes, I do. No, I don't. Half a second. It was on his card. Oh, I know! Inspector Brown. Quiet, plain sort of chap."

Ritz Hotel

## Chapter 6 — A Plan of Campaign

It turned out that Scotland Yard had no record of an Inspector Brown, and there were no more copies of Jane Finn's photograph. Thus, the Young Adventurers were off to a bad start, but it could have been worse, because they moved into the Ritz hotel, best in London, in Tommy's words, "To be closer to the only living relative of Jane Finn."

However, even after three days of good meals and much debate, Tuppence and Tommy had to admit they were stuck. But Tuppence suddenly had a bright idea.

"We have the name Rita. Whittington mentioned it. Danvers was followed on the ship, wasn't he? I'm betting it was by a woman. That *could* have been Rita. She must have survived. Otherwise how would Mr. Brown have known about Danvers? We only need to search the list of survivors for her."

"Hm. So you just need the list. Carry on Sherlock Holmes."

"I already asked Mr. Carter for the list and here it is."

Both Young Adventurers set to work reading through the list.

"This is more complicated than I thought!" Tommy said. "There are very few first names for the women."

"Then we just have to visit all of them and find out which one is Rita. We'll start with all the women in London."

Tommy hit on the bright idea of pretending he was checking names for the Borough Voting Registers. They had collected a Gladys, a Mary and become confused by a change of address before they arrived at South Audley Mansions. This was an imposing–looking block of flats just off Park Lane. No. 20 was on the second floor. Tommy gave his story about the Voting Register to the maid and asked the first name of the woman that lived there.

"Margaret."

Tommy spelt it, but the other interrupted him.

"No, G U E."

"Oh, Marguerite; spelt the French way, I see." He paused, then plunged in boldly. "We had her down as Rita Vandemeyer, but I suppose that's incorrect?"

"She's mostly called that, sir, but Marguerite's her name."

"Thank you. That's all. Good morning."

Hardly able to contain his excitement, Tommy hurried down the stairs. Tuppence was waiting at the angle of the turn.

"You heard?"

"Yes. Oh, Tommy!"

Tommy squeezed her arm back.

Suddenly, to Tommy's complete surprise, Tuppence dragged him into the little space by the side of the lift where the shadow was deepest.

"What the—"

"Hush!"

Two men came down the stairs and passed out through the entrance. Tuppence's hand closed tighter on Tommy's arm.

"Quick—follow them. I daren't. He might recognize me. I don't know who the other man is, but the bigger of the two was Whittington."

# Chapter 7 — The House in Soho

The two men walked quite quickly, so Tommy had no trouble holding back far enough that they wouldn't notice him. They reached Oxford Street, turned right and entered a restaurant. Tommy followed them in and took a table next to theirs, ignoring Whittington for now and taking in the appearance of the smaller man.

He was fair-haired, and his eyes, small and crafty, shifted unceasingly.

Tommy thought the blonde man was either Polish or Russian. The only word Tommy picked out from their conversation was "Ireland;" but it seemed that the big man was giving orders. Whittington called the other man Boris.

Suddenly, a crowd of people at the next table left and Tommy heard the name "Mr. Brown" clearly. The blonde man laughed and replied:

"Why not, my friend? It is a respectable name—very common. Did he not choose it for that reason? Ah, I should like to meet him—Mr. Brown."

There was a steely ring in Whittington's voice as he replied:

"Who knows? You may have met him already."

"Bah!" replied the other. "That is baby talk—a fable for the police. Do you know what I say to myself sometimes? That he is a fable invented by the Inner Ring, a bogeyman to frighten us with. It might be so."

"We may as well go."

Whittington paid the waitress and led the other man to the pavement, where they hailed a cab. Luckily for Tommy, another one came along, right behind. He hailed it by raising his hand and ordered the driver to:

"Follow that cab."

Whittington ended his journey at Waterloo railway station. He and the man went straight to the ticket office, but they didn't notice Tommy standing right behind them. Whittington bought a ticket to Bournemouth, so Tommy did the same. As he emerged, Boris said, glancing up at the clock: "You are early. You have nearly half an hour."

Tommy suddenly realised that the blonde man wasn't going with Whittington. This presented a problem. How could Tommy follow both? He thought of calling

Tuppence, but she was too far away. Instead, he noted where the men were standing and rushed for the nearest telephone.

Tommy called up the Ritz and asked for Julius Hersheimmer. There was a click and a buzz. Oh, if only the young American was in his room! There was another click, and then "Hello" in unmistakable accents came over the wire.

"That you, Hersheimmer? Beresford speaking. I'm at Waterloo. I've followed Whittington and another man here. No time to explain. Whittington's off to Bournemouth by the 3.30. Can you get there by then?"

The reply was reassuring.

"Sure. I'll hustle."

The telephone rang off. Tommy put back the receiver with a sigh of relief. He knew that the American would hustle enough to arrive in time. Whittington and Boris were still where he had left them. Tommy fingered his pocket thoughtfully. In spite of Carter's permission to spend whatever was necessary, the first–class ticket to Bournemouth had left him with only a dollar in his pocket. He hoped that Julius would arrive with more.

In the meantime, the minutes were creeping by: 3.15, 3.20, 3.25, 3.27. Supposing Julius did not get there in time? 3.29 .... Doors were banging. Tommy felt cold waves of despair pass over him. Then a hand fell on his shoulder.

"Here I am, son. Your British traffic beats description! Put me wise to the crooks right away."

"That's Whittington—there, getting in now, that big dark man. The other is Boris, the foreign chap he's talking to."

"I'm on to them. Which of the two is mine?"

Tommy had thought out this question.

"Got any money with you?"

Julius shook his head, and Tommy's face fell.

"I guess I haven't more than three or four hundred dollars with me at the moment," explained the American.

Tommy gave a faint whoop of relief.

"Oh, Lord, you millionaires! You don't talk the same language! Get on the train. Here's your ticket. Whittington's your man."

"Got it! So long Tommy."

Tommy drew a deep breath. Boris was coming along the platform towards him.

Tommy allowed him to pass and then took up the chase once more. From Waterloo Boris took the tube as far as Piccadilly Circus. Then he walked up Shaftesbury Avenue, finally turning off into the maze of mean streets round Soho. Tommy followed him at a safe distance.

They eventually reached a small, run-down house, just off a square. From the shelter of a doorway Tommy watched Boris go up the steps of a particularly evil–looking house and rap sharply, with a peculiar rhythm, on the door. It was opened quickly, he said a word or two to the door-keeper, then passed inside.

It was at this moment that Tommy lost his head. He should have waited patiently where he was for his man to come out again. Instead, he walked straight up to the house and copied Boris's knock. The door swung open, and a nasty looking man with close–cropped hair stood in the doorway.

"Well?" he grunted.

Tommy suddenly felt scared. He said the first words that came into his mind.

"Mr. Brown?" he said.

To his surprise the man stood aside.

"Upstairs," he said, jerking his thumb over his shoulder, "second door on your left."

# Chapter 8 — The Adventures of Tommy

Surprised, Tommy climbed the stairs and heard a low murmur of voices from the room. He noticed a small recess immediately on his right, half concealed by a torn velvet curtain, which gave a good view of the staircase and door. Tommy hesitated.

"They will quickly know I'm not one of them," Tommy thought. "I know nothing! If they ask me another password, I'll be caught!"

A repetition of the signal knock sounded on the door below, and Tommy, his mind made up, slipped quickly into the recess and drew the curtain. There were several slits in the ancient material which gave him a good view. He would watch events, and any time he chose could, after all, join the assembly, copying the last arrival.

The man, square-jawed and wearing scruffy clothes, knocked. The door opened and for a moment Tommy could see that five men sat around a table, looking at a man with close-cropped hair and a short, pointed, naval–looking beard. He asked the new arrival:

"Your number, comrade?"

"Fourteen, gov'nor," replied the other hoarsely.

"Correct." The door shut again.

Two more men arrived, the last, a short man whose eyes reminded Tommy of a snake's. He peered at the curtain, making Tommy shiver, but then he knocked on the door. It opened.

"We are honoured," a German-sounding voice said. "We are greatly honoured. I much feared that it would be impossible."

The other answered in a low voice that had a kind of hiss in it:

"There were difficulties. It will not be possible again, I fear. But one meeting is essential—to define my policy. I can do nothing without—Mr. Brown. He is here?"

"We have received a message. It is impossible for him to be present in person."

The voice stopped, giving a curious impression of having left the sentence unfinished.

"So be it. Let's proceed. Perhaps Number Fourteen will shut the door?"

Tommy listened hard, but once the door had shut he could hear nothing. He was just to leave when he heard the sound of chairs scraping across wooden floorboards. Two voices rose as the meeting drew to a close.

"And—the date, my friend?"

"The 29th. The general strike has to happen on that day. Then, public opinion will be with the labour unions! And us!"

But Tommy heard no more. Suddenly something heavy crashed down on the back of his head.

# Chapter 9 — Tuppence Enters Domestic Service

When Tommy left, Tuppence didn't know what to do next. She was just about to leave the block of luxury apartments when she noticed a lift-boy in a smart suit, polishing the brass bannister in the entrance lobby. She walked up to him casually and said:

"Well William, getting a good shine?"

The lift-boy grinned and corrected her. "Albert miss."

She had noticed a cheap crime thriller novel sticking out of Albert's pocket, so she decided to try and get his help.

"Know what this is?"

Tuppence pulled back her coat to reveal an enamel nursing badge. She didn't wait for Albert to guess.

"American Detective Force," Tuppence replied, putting on her best American accent.

"Wow! Really? Are you on a case?"

"No. 20. Calls herself Vandemeyer. Ha! ha!"

"A crook?"

"Ready Rita they call her in America."

"Ready Rita! Wow! Annie always said she was bad!"

"Annie?"

"Her maid. She's leaving today. Rita's a stunner, isn't she?"

"Sure is! Diamonds. That's what she stole. But we'll catch her."

"Can I help?"

"Not at the moment, but I might think of something. What's with this Annie?"

"They had a big bust-up. Annie's been told to leave. But the Lady won't find somebody to replace her easily."

"Oh, won't she? Do you think you could tell her you have a cousin who is a first-class maid?"

"I get you! Great idea. I'll mention it right away, casual like."

"Tell her I'll come at eleven tomorrow morning."

"Right. Where do I contact you?"

"Ritz. Name of Cowley."

"Wow! Must pay well, being a detective!"

Tuppence went back to her hotel room, but there was no word from Tommy. Disappointed, she went shopping, buying a lot of clothes, a maid's uniform and a blonde wig. By the time she had finished and looked at her reflection in the mirror, she knew not even Tommy would recognise her. She sent a brief note to Mr. Carter and went to bed.

The following morning brought a reply from Carter.

> My Dear Miss. Cowley,
> You will find everything arranged.
> You have lived for two years with
> Miss Dufferin, The Parsonage,
> Llanelly, and Mrs. Vandemeyer
> can apply to her for a reference.
> May I give a word or two of ad-
> vice? Stick as near to the truth as
> possible—it minimizes the danger
> of slip-ups.
> Good luck.
> Carter

There was no word from Tommy, but the post brought a scruffy postcard with the words "It's O.K." scrawled on it.

It was a few minutes past eleven when Tuppence again entered the hall of South Audley Mansions. Albert was on the look–out, attending to his duties in a careless way. He did not immediately recognize Tuppence. When he did, his admiration was obvious.

"Blessed if I'd have known you! That disguise is amazing!"

"Glad you like it, Albert," replied Tuppence modestly. "By the way, am I your cousin or am I not?"

"Your voice too," cried the delighted boy. "It's as English as anything! No, I said as a friend of mine knew a young gal."

"I've come about the place," said Tuppence, when she reached the door to the apartment.

Tuppence stopped when she saw Mrs. Vandemeyer for the first time. Tall and elegant, not young but clearly a woman who had once been a great beauty and with eyes of electric blue, the woman had a kind of metallic strength that came out in the tones of her voice and in that piercing quality of her eyes.

For the first time Tuppence felt afraid. She felt that fooling this woman would be very different to fooling Whittington.

"You can sit down. How did you hear I wanted a housemaid?"

"Through a friend who knows the lift-boy here. He thought the place might suit me." Again, that steely glance seemed to pierce her right through. "You speak like an educated girl?"

Tuppence ran through her imaginary career according to Mr. Carter's advice. She stuck mainly to the facts, mentioning that she had worked in a hospital. It seemed to her, as she did so, that Mrs. Vandemeyer relaxed.

"Good," replied Mrs. Vandemeyer. "And a reference?"

Tuppence gave the address for the reference, and then Mrs. Vandemeyer said:

"I will pay you $80 per week. You can send for your things using my telephone, and I will show you to your room. What's your name?"

"Prudence Cooper, ma'am."

# Chapter 10 — Enter Sir James Peel Edgerton

Having the hospital Tuppence was very confident in her abilities as a housemaid. She didn't have to wait long to be tested. That very evening a guest arrived.

At a few minutes past eight the front door bell rang, and Tuppence went to answer it with some nervousness. She was relieved to see that the visitor was the second of the two men whom Tommy had followed.

He gave his name as Count Stepanov. Tuppence announced him, and Mrs. Vandemeyer rose from her low sofa with a quick murmur of pleasure.

"It is delightful to see you, Boris Ivanovitch," she said.

"And you, madame!"

He bowed low over her hand. After serving the first course Tuppence listened at the door.

"She's new," said the Count. "Quite safe, I suppose?"

"Really, Boris, you are so suspicious. I believe she's the cousin of the hall porter, or something of the kind. And nobody even dreams that I have any connection with our—mutual friend, Mr. Brown. Peel Edgerton doesn't."

"You will end by ruining us! Peel Edgerton is perhaps, the most celebrated lawyer in England, but his special hobby is hunting criminals! It is madness!"

"I know he has saved untold men from hanging," said Mrs. Vandemeyer calmly.

"You are a clever woman, Rita; but you are also a fool! Be guided by me and give up Peel Edgerton."

"I will not."

"Then we will make you!"

"You forget, Boris," she said. "I answer to no one, except—Mr. Brown."

"Sometimes I believe that you would sell—us!"

"The price would have to be very big," she said lightly.

Tuppence had left a message for Tommy to send letters to a local post office, where Albert could pick them up. But the following morning Albert said there had been nothing. Now Tuppence felt very worried about Tommy.

"What day do you normally take off?" Mrs. Vandemeyer asked Tuppence just after breakfast.

"Friday, ma'am."

"Today is Friday. You may take today off."

Tuppence was just about to go to her room to change when the doorbell rang. She opened the door to a man who looked very important. Just a shade over average height, he still seemed like a big man, stronger than most. She couldn't take her eyes off of him. He gave her his name: Sir James Peel Edgerton.

Half an hour later the bell rang, telling Tuppence it was time to show the visitor out. But he stopped outside the door and said:

"Not been doing this long, have you."

"No, sir."

"Good place here?"

"Very good, thank you, sir."

"Ah, but there are plenty of good places nowadays. And a change does no harm sometimes."

"Do you mean—?" began Tuppence.

But Sir James had already turned and began to walk away. Tuppence heard him say over his shoulder:

"Just a hint. That's all."

## Chapter 11 —Julius Tells A Story

When Tuppence reached the Ritz, she wasn't surprized to learn that Tommy still hadn't returned. She was told that Julius Hersheimmer was out, but he returned, out of breath, a few minutes later.

"Hello Miss. Cowley. Tommy here?"

"No. Do you know where he is?"

"What! He hasn't returned!"

"You don't know where he is?" she asked faintly.

"I? How should I know? I haven't had one darned word from him, though I wired him yesterday morning."

"I expect your wire's at the office unopened."

"Where is he then?"

"I don't know. I hoped you might."

"Not seen him since Waterloo."

"Waterloo?"

"He called me and told me to hustle down to Waterloo station. I joined him seconds before a train left. He stuck a ticket for Bournemouth in my hand and told me to follow this chap called Whittington. Which I did! Tommy chased after a guy called Boris with blonde hair. He looked Russian."

"Oh! What happened next?"

"To cut a long story short, I followed Whittington to a big place, just on the edge of town—you know, long lawn, lots of trees, three or four floors. I waited until after dark for him to come out, but no dice. I snuck around the back and tried to peer in the windows. A light came on the second floor, and I desperately wanted to see inside, so I climbed a tree. I had to shimmy along a branch to get close enough to the window." Hersheimmer paused for effect.

"What did you see?"

"Well, I saw *him*, talking to a nurse. She seemed to be answering questions. He seemed very determined—once or twice he beat with his fist on the table. The rain had stopped now, and the sky was clearing in that sudden way it does. The moon came out, and I was worried they might see me, so I backed along the branch, and it broke!"

"Oh no!"

"A few scratches, nothing much. But the bad bit is that I must have knocked myself out! I woke in a bed. A little man with glasses and a black beard was looking after me."

"'I am Dr. Hall, and this is my private nursing home,' he said. 'You had a nasty fall, but the only damage seems to be a sprained ankle. You fell out of one of my trees! What were you doing there?' I wanted to get out immediately, but I had to have an answer, so I decided to play it cool. 'I lost a girl I was protecting. I thought she was in your building. Jane Finn's the name. Have you seen or heard of her?' He repeated the name and said he hadn't seen her."

"Did you leave then?"

"Well, no, because I had seen Whittington, I asked Dr. Hall about him, pretending that he was an old friend. Hall told me that Whittington had come down to visit his niece, Nurse Edith, but that they had both gone back to London. I even asked for Whittington's address. He said he didn't have it but could write to the nurse. I hadn't found out much, so I left and came straight back here. You look very pale, Miss. Tuppence!"

"I'm so worried about Tommy. I saw Boris at Vandemeyer's and I think something bad might have happened to Tommy. I've written to Carter for his help."

"You saw Boris?"

Tuppence told Hersheimmer all about her time in Mrs. Vandemeyer's apartment. He was impressed.

"You're a mighty brave little lady!" Hersheimmer said. "Well, we can't do much here. Maybe we should stake out Mrs. Vandemeyer's apartment and see if Boris turns up again."

"Yes, that's probably a good idea. We need cover though."

"No problem. I was thinking of buying a car. Any suggestions? Something good."

Tuppence said the only car manufacturer's name that she could think of:

"Rolls Royce."

"Done! Get ready. I will be back with the car in half an hour."

"But you can't just buy one like that! You have to wait years for a Rolls Royce."

"Don't you worry. Money can work magic!"

Half an hour was almost up when a lift-boy knocked on Tuppence's door and told her a man was waiting for her outside in a Rolls Royce.

As the newly appointed chauffeur drove to Mrs. Vandemeyer's apartment, Tuppence told Julius about Sir James Peel Edgerton's warning.

"But why would he do that?" Julius said.

"I don't know," confessed Tuppence. "But he looked kind, and very clever. I wouldn't mind going to him and telling him everything."

"See here," he said, "we don't want any lawyers mixed up in this. That guy couldn't help us any."

# Chapter 12 — A Friend In Need

Friday and Saturday passed quietly. Tuppence had received a brief answer from Mr. Carter. In it he pointed out that the Young Adventurers had undertaken the work at their own risk and had been fully warned of the dangers. He couldn't help them.

This was cold comfort for Tuppence, whose concern for Tommy had grown. But she reminded herself that:

"He might be slow, but he is very sure."

While Tuppence worked inside the apartment, Julius waited outside in the car, but Boris never came.

Tuppence could only think of asking Peel Edgerton for help.

"There's nobody else!" she pleaded with Julius.

Eventually the American gave in and they drove to Carlton House Terrace, which Tuppence had found in a directory of English lawyers as Peel Edgerton's address.

"Will you ask Sir James if I can see him for a few minutes?" Tuppence asked the butler. "I have an important message for him."

The butler left, returning a moment or two later.

"Sir James will see you now."

He showed them into a library at the back of the house. Tuppence noticed that all one wall was devoted to works on crime. There were several deep–padded leather arm–chairs, and an old–fashioned fireplace. In front of the window was a big roll–top desk covered with papers at which the master of the house was sitting.

He rose as they entered.

"You have a message for me? Ah"—he recognized Tuppence with a smile—"it's you, is it? Brought a message from Mrs. Vandemeyer, I suppose?"

"Not exactly," said Tuppence. "In fact, I'm afraid I only said that to be quite sure of getting in. Oh, by the way, this is Mr. Hersheimmer, Sir James Peel Edgerton."

"Pleased to meet you," said the American, shooting out a hand.

"Won't you both sit down?" asked Sir James.

He drew forward two chairs.

"Sir James," said Tuppence, plunging boldly, "I dare say you will think it's rude of me coming here like this. Because, of course, it's nothing whatever to do with you, and then you're a very important person, and of course Tommy and I are very unimportant." She paused for breath.

"Tommy?" queried Sir James, looking across at the American.

"No, that's Julius," explained Tuppence. "I'm rather nervous, and that makes me tell it badly. What I really want to know is what you meant by what you said to me the other day? Did you mean to warn me against Mrs. Vandemeyer? You did, didn't you?"

"My dear young lady, as far as I remember I only mentioned that there were equally good jobs to be had elsewhere."

"Yes, I know. But it was a hint, wasn't it?"

"Well, perhaps it was," admitted Sir James gravely.

"Well, I want to know more. I want to know just *why* you gave me a hint."

Sir James smiled at her honesty.

"Well, if I had a young sister forced to earn her living, I would not like to see her in Mrs. Vandemeyer's service. I felt it my duty just to give you a hint. It is no place for a young and inexperienced girl. That is all I can tell you."

"But I'm not experienced, and I know that she's bad. Shall I tell him all Julius?"

"I'd go right ahead with the facts," replied the American.

Tuppence told the whole story, from beginning to end.

"Very interesting," Sir James said, when she finished. "A great deal of what you tell me, child, is already known to me. I've had certain theories of my own about this Jane Finn. You've done very well so far, but it's rather too bad of—what do you know him as?—Mr. Carter to pitchfork you two young things into an affair of this kind. By the way, where did Mr. Hersheimmer come in originally? You didn't make that clear?"

Julius answered for himself. "I'm Jane's first cousin," he explained, returning the lawyer's keen gaze.

"Ah!"

"Oh, Sir James," broke out Tuppence, "what do you think has become of Tommy?"

"When you arrived, young lady, I was just packing my bags. Going to Scotland by the night train for a few days' fishing. But there are different kinds of fishing. I might stay and see if we can get on the track of that young chap."

"Oh!" said Tuppence, clapping her hands.

"Now, don't get too excited, Miss—"

"Cowley. Prudence Cowley. But my friends call me Tuppence."

"Now, about this young Tommy of yours. Frankly, things look bad for him. He's been butting in somewhere where he wasn't wanted. No doubt of it. But don't give up hope. He may have valuable information, so we must find him."

"Yes, but how?" cried Tuppence. "I've tried to think of everything."

Sir James smiled. "And yet there's one person quite near at hand who probably knows where he is, or at least where he is likely to be."

"Who is that?" asked Tuppence, puzzled.

"Mrs. Vandemeyer."

"Yes, but she'd never tell us."

"Ah, that is where I come in. I think that I shall be able to make Mrs. Vandemeyer tell me what I want to know."

"How?" demanded Tuppence, opening her eyes very wide.

"Oh, just by asking her questions," replied Sir James easily. "That's the way we do it, you know. But if she won't, there is always the possibility of bribery."

"Sure. And that's where I come in!" cried Julius, bringing his fist down on the table with a bang. "You can count on me, if necessary, for one million dollars!"

"You really can! He's that rich!" Tuppence added.

"I see," Sir James said, sitting down with a dazed look on his face. "There is no time to be lost. The sooner we strike the better." He turned to Tuppence. "Is Mrs. Vandemeyer dining out to–night, do you know?"

"Yes, I think so, but she will not be out late. Otherwise, she would have taken the key."

"Good. I will call upon her about ten o'clock. What time are you supposed to return?"

"About nine–thirty or ten, but I could go back earlier."

"No. That might look strange. Be back by nine–thirty. Mr. Hersheimmer will wait below in a cab perhaps."

"He's got a new Rolls–Royce car," said Tuppence with pride.

"Even better. If I succeed in getting the address from her, we can go there at once, taking Mrs. Vandemeyer with us if necessary. You understand?"

"Yes," the both replied, together.

"Now, Miss Tuppence, my advice to you is to go and have a good dinner, a *really* good one, mind. And don't think ahead more than you can help." He shook hands with them both, and a moment later they were outside.

"Isn't he wonderful?" inquired Tuppence, skipping down the steps.

Rolls Royce

# Chapter 13 — The Vigil

Tuppence had too much energy to eat right away, so she went for a walk around Hyde Park, but by six o'clock she was wondering all the time what was happening at South Audley Mansions. It wasn't far away, so she decided to take a look. Nothing had changed. The building looked the same, and everything seemed quiet. She was just turning away when she heard a piercing whistle, and the faithful Albert came running from the building to join her.

Tuppence frowned. It wasn't her plan to be seen, but Albert was purple with excitement.

"I say, miss, she's going!"

"Who's going?" demanded Tuppence sharply.

"Ready Rita. Mrs. Vandemeyer. She's packing up, and she's just sent down word for me to get her a cab."

"What?" Tuppence clutched his arm.

"It's the truth, miss. I thought maybe you didn't know about it."

"Albert," cried Tuppence, "you're a star. If it hadn't been for you we'd have lost her. Is there a telephone around here?"

"Just around the corner?"

"Go to it then, at once, and ring up the Ritz Hotel. Ask for Mr. Hersheimmer, and when you get him tell him to get Sir James and come on at once, as Mrs. Vandemeyer is trying to get away. If you can't get him, ring up Sir James Peel Edgerton, you'll find his number in the book, and tell him what's happening. You won't forget the names, will you?"

"No miss. Don't worry!"

Tuppence ran up the steps and pressed the bell firmly. She might learn something from the cook. She heard footsteps inside, and a moment later Mrs. Vandemeyer herself opened the door. She lifted her eyebrows at the sight of the girl.

"You?"

"I had a touch of toothache, ma'am," said Tuppence, "so thought it better to come home and have a quiet evening."

Mrs. Vandemeyer said nothing, but she drew back and let Tuppence pass into the hall. In a flash, a rim of cold steel touched her temple, and Mrs. Vandemeyer's voice rose cold and menacing:

"You little fool! Do you think I don't know? No, don't answer. If you struggle or cry out, I'll shoot you like a dog. Now march! Into my room. By the time I've finished you will sleep and not feel any toothache at all!"

Tuppence didn't like the sound of this. But the gun barrel against her temple convinced her she had to go along with Rita's orders, at least for now. The room was a mess. Clothes were everywhere.

Mrs. Vandemeyer laid down the revolver on the edge of the washstand within reach of her hand, and, still eyeing Tuppence like a lynx in case the girl should attempt to move, she took a little stoppered bottle from its place on the marble and poured some of its contents into a glass which she filled up with water.

"What's that?" asked Tuppence sharply.

"Something to make you sleep. Drink this."

"No! It might be poison!"

"It's just to make you sleep. I don't have time to tie you up or dispose of a body."

In her heart Tuppence believed her, but if she slept then Rita would escape. Tuppence thought quickly. In a flash, she saw a chance, a very dangerous chance. She threw herself on the floor and begged for mercy.

"Get up, you little idiot!"

Tuppence raised a trembling left hand to the glass.

"Very well." Her mouth opened meekly.

Mrs. Vandemeyer sighed with relief, off her guard for the moment. Then, quick as a flash, Tuppence jerked the glass upward as hard as she could. The fluid in it splashed into Mrs. Vandemeyer's face, and during her momentary gasp, Tuppence's right hand shot out and grasped the revolver where it lay on the edge of the washstand.

In the moment of victory, Tuppence couldn't help herself. "Now who's on top and who's underneath?" she crowed.

"Not a fool, then, after all! Very good. But you can't succeed!"

"Let's talk."

"What about?" said Mrs. Vandemeyer.

Tuppence eyed her thoughtfully for a minute. She was remembering several things.

"I heard Boris's words, 'I believe you would sell—us!' and your answer, 'The price would have to be enormous.' How about two hundred thousand dollars?"

A flush crept over Mrs. Vandemeyer's
face. "What did you say?" she asked, her
fingers playing nervously with a brooch on
her breast.

Tuppence repeated the amount.

The light died out of Mrs. Vandemeyer's
eyes. She leaned back in her chair. "Bah!"
she said. "You haven't got it."

"No," admitted Tuppence, "I haven't—
but I know someone who has."

"Who?"

"An American millionaire."

Mrs. Vandemeyer sat up.

"I think I believe you. What does your
friend want to know?"

"Where is Jane Finn?"

"I'm not sure where she is at the present
moment," she replied.

"But you could find out?"

"Oh, yes," returned Mrs. Vandemeyer
carelessly. "That would not be a problem."

"There's a boy, a friend of mine. I'm
afraid something's happened to him,
through your pal Boris."

"What's his name?"

"Tommy Beresford."

"Never heard of him. But I'll ask Boris.
He'll tell me anything he knows."

"There's one more thing. Who is *Mr. Brown*?"

Mrs. Vandemeyer shrugged her shoulders.

"You can't have learned much about us if you don't know that *nobody knows* who Mr. Brown is."

"*You* do."

Again, the colour left the other's face.

"What makes you think that?"

"I don't know," said the girl truthfully. "But I'm sure of it."

"Yes," she said hoarsely, at last, "I know. I was beautiful, you see—very beautiful—"

"You are still," said Tuppence.

Mrs. Vandemeyer shook her head. There was a strange gleam in her electric–blue eyes.

"Not beautiful enough," she said in a soft, dangerous tone. "I will do all that you ask. What was that?"

"What?"

"I heard a noise!"

"You don't know him," she reiterated hoarsely. "He's—ah!"

With a shriek of terror, she sprang to her feet. Her outstretched hand pointed over Tuppence's head. Then she fainted and fell to the floor. Tuppence looked round to see what had startled her. In the doorway were Sir James Peel Edgerton and Julius Hersheimmer.

Sir James brushed past Julius and quickly felt Mrs. Vandemeyer's brow.

"Heart!" he said "Must be shock. Get some brandy."

Together, he and Tuppence lifted the woman onto the bed while Julius fetched the drink. Soon Mr's. Vandemeyer opened her eyes and tried to speak.

"Don't talk!" Sir James told her. "Lie still."

All three moved to the corridor to talk. Tuppence explained her offer to Rita, to which both Sir James and Julius nodded.

"But I can't get the money until morning!" Julius replied.

"Oh! We'll have to wait then. There's no way out of that room. The balcony doesn't extend that far. We can lock her in and wait until morning."

"Good idea!" Sir James said.

"She is terrified Mr. Brown will murder her!" Tuppence explained.

"We'll have to take turns Julius," Sir James suggested, "keeping guard on the room. He won't get in!"

Tuppence went to check on their prisoner before they locked the room.

"Don't—leave—" Mrs. Vandemeyer seemed unable to say any more, only murmuring something that sounded like "sleepy." Then she tried again. Tuppence bent lower still. It was only a breath. "Mr.—Brown—" The voice stopped.

They locked the door from the outside and Tuppence slept in her own bed while the two men kept watch until morning. Julius woke her with a cup of tea.

"We drink coffee in America!" he said. "But this will have to do."

"Thank you. How is our patient?"

"We're just about to check on her. How did you sleep?"

"Not well. I can't help feeling that Mr. Brown's somewhere in the flat! I can *feel* him."

"Nonsense! But I tell you something Sir James told me that's interesting. I asked where he thought Jane was now. He said he didn't know, but he knew where she had been. He said that nurse I saw in Dr. Hall's nursing home must have been her! He also thinks Dr. Hall is in on it! Imagine! I actually saw her and I didn't know it! I could kick myself. Let's go."

The two men stood behind her while Tuppence unlocked Mrs. Vandemeyer's bedroom door. She stepped over to the bed and shook the woman's shoulders before drawing the curtains. But when she turned around, Mrs. Vandemeyer hadn't moved. Tuppence felt her wrist.

"Cold as ice!" she cried.

"Dead!" Sir James said.

"By jiminy!" Julius said.

Sir James called a doctor while the other two searched the room for anything of use to the investigation. Julius found a safe, which lay open.

"Anything inside?" Tuppence asked.

Julius seemed to hesitate before replying, "No."

The doctor declared Accidental Death by Overdose after they found that the bottle of sleeping powder was now completely empty.

# Chapter 14 — A Consultation

Sir James took care of all the official paperwork for the dead woman and suggested they visit his friend, Dr. Hall. The doctor was very surprised to see Julius again so soon after his fall from the tree. Sir James told the doctor of Mrs. Vandemeyer's death, to which the doctor replied:

"She's dead! How sad. A very beautiful woman and a very good friend of mine."

"Dr. Hall, did Mrs. Vandemeyer ever bring a relative of hers to you in Bournemouth?"

"Why yes! A long time ago. It was June or July of 1915. She said the girl, her niece, had been on the Lusitania when it was sunk and lost her memory from the shock. If you want a statement from her, I should warn you that she can remember nothing before the sinking on May 7, 1915."

"Pity. That is a great pity," Sir James said.

"It is really a matter of waiting," Dr. Hall replied.

"Waiting?"

"Yes, sooner or later, the memory will return—as suddenly as it went. But in all probability the girl will have completely forgotten the period in between and will take up life where she left off—at the sinking of the Lusitania."

"And when do you expect this to happen?"

The doctor shrugged his shoulders.

"It could be tomorrow or in ten years' time. There's no way of knowing. A sudden shock can sometimes bring it back."

"Can we at least see her?" Julius asked.

"See her? Didn't I explain? She left my care a few days ago."

# Chapter 15 — Tuppence Receives A Proposal

"When did you last see her"? Julius asked.

"The evening you fell out of my tree! A message came from Mrs. Vandemeyer. The young lady and her nurse left on a train shortly after you left."

Julius sank back again into his chair.

"I was such a fool!" the American declared. "Such a fool. She was there! Within my grasp!"

Tuppence was just about to ask the doctor more questions when Sir James gave her a warning glance. They left without speaking much more on the matter.

"What do we do now?" asked Tuppence.

"You must hope for the best," Sir James said. "I'm going away. To Scotland. Any letters you send will be sent on to me."

"Oh!"

Tuppence felt hopeless.

"You mustn't give up!" Sir James told her. "Holiday time doesn't mean one can do no work at all."

They left Sir James in London and Julius drove Tuppence back to the Ritz. He

noticed how quiet she had become and
asked her:

"You really miss Mr. Beresford. Are you
two in love?"

"Us? Oh no! We have been friends since
we were children. That's all."

"Well, suppose he's—well—suppose this
doesn't work out well."

"Say it! Suppose he's *dead*!"

"I didn't want to say it. But what will
you do then? You'll be mighty lonesome, a
sweet kid like you on your own."

"I shall be alright," Tuppence replied,
sniffing.

"What about marriage? Got any views on
the subject?"

"I intend to marry, of course," replied
Tuppence. "That is, if"—she paused and
then stuck to her guns bravely—"I can find
someone rich enough to make it worth my
while. That's honest, isn't it? I dare say you
hate me for it."

"I never look down on business matters.
What figure did you have in mind?"

"What do you mean? Height? Or
money?"

"Money. How about me?"

"You? Oh, I couldn't!"

"Why not?"

"I can't," gasped Tuppence.

"Because of Beresford?"

"No, no, *no!*"

"Well then?"

Tuppence only continued to shake her head violently.

"I'd be grateful if you'd do me the favour of thinking it over until tomorrow."

"It's no use."

"Let's leave it like that."

Neither of them spoke again until they reached the Ritz. Tuppence went upstairs to her room. She felt morally battered to the ground by Julius's pushy personality. Sitting down in front of the glass, she stared at her own reflection for some minutes.

"Fool," murmured Tuppence at length, making a grimace. "Little fool. Everything you want—"

But then she saw the photograph of Tommy that she always kept. Struggling to control herself she suddenly held it to her lips and burst into tears.

"Oh Tommy! I *do* love you! Where are you?"

After wiping her eyes, she suddenly realised she had to think what to say to Julius.

"He's so American! I wonder if he did find anything in that safe."

Tuppence felt shocked at the thoughts that entered her head.

"Impossible," she murmured. "Impossible! I must be going mad even to think of such a thing … . And yet it explains everything!"

Tuppence wrote a short note, walked to Julius's door and tapped on it. He didn't reply, so she tried the door handle. Finding it unlocked she stepped inside and left the note for him. She had just closed the door again when a boy called to her.

"Telegram for you, miss!"

"Tommy!"

# Chapter 16 — Further Adventures of Tommy

Julius had arrived to take a meal in the Ritz restaurant when Tommy walked up to him and sat down.

"Holy snakes!" Julius said. "is it really you?"

"Of course. Why wouldn't it be?"

"We thought you were dead man!"

"Who?"

"Tuppence and I. Where have you been?"

"Ah! There's a long story, but I must eat something first. I haven't had a proper meal for more than four days!"

Over the hors d'oeuvres, Tommy told Julius about his adventure in Soho and being knocked out. He told the rest of the story over a main course, although the American forgot to eat most of the food placed before him as he listened, amazed.

"When I at last opened my eyes, I was conscious of nothing but a terrible pain through my temples. I think I swore, and a German man told me to drink some water. To cut a long story short, they said they were going to kill me, but they wanted some answers first. I told them how I got in, but then I added that they couldn't kill me, because I knew too much, for instance the password."

"You were so brave lad—and clever!"

"The German was very angry. He pushed over a few chairs and threatened to throttle me right there. I managed to smile at him, as if I didn't believe it. I knew my only chance was to bluff my way out. Anyway, I had to think hard. Then I came up with the bright idea of offering them the Danvers top-secret papers."

"But you don't have them!"
"No, but they didn't know that! Anyway, I had their agreement to let me go, as long as one of their men went with me. But then something happened. I asked to see Jane Finn and ask her some questions. They laughed! I don't understand why they laughed. Then they locked me up."

# Chapter 17 — Annette

"My prison was filthy dirty, had no windows, very little furniture and no decoration, except four pictures of scenes from Faust: Marguerite with her box of jewels, Faust and Mephistopheles and two others," Tommy continued, "but luckily they made this girl bring me my food."

"Was she pretty?"

"Very. Her hair was a full rich brown, with sudden glints of gold in it as though there were imprisoned sunbeams struggling in its depths. There was a wild–rose quality about her face. Her eyes, set wide apart, were hazel, a golden hazel that again recalled a memory of sunbeams."

"She sounds like a real beauty."

"I had a sudden idea and asked her if she was Jane Finn. She said that her name was Annette. She spoke English with a soft, French accent and called me 'monsieur."

"I see."

"I asked her why she was in the house— but she seemed afraid and left very quickly. The next time she came I tried to get her to help me escape. She told me they were 'her people' and that she couldn't do it, but I knew she was afraid of them. Then she asked if I had come to save Jane Finn. I told her yes, and this made her smile. Nothing happened until the evening of the third day after this."

"What happened then?"

"Well, the doorman, whose name, I learned, was Conrad, came with another man and they started to tie me up. They told me they were going to get rid of my body the following morning. I asked how they would kill me, but they only laughed. Then Conrad said that I wasn't at the Ritz anymore. How did he know where I was staying?"

Julius thought he knew the answer to two of Tommy's questions now, and though he didn't want to tell him just yet, he could barely stop himself.

"Are you alright?" Tommy asked. "You haven't eaten a thing!"

"I'm fine. Carry on."

"You're not saying much. Alright. Well, they left, and I could see no hope anywhere. About an hour had passed when I heard the key softly turned, and the door opened. It was Annette. Conrad called her back, but she told him she had to turn out the lights. To my amazement I felt her running her hands over my bonds. She slipped something cold and hard into my hand and left. It was a knife!"

"Hm. Perhaps she's not so bad after all."

"Hm. Anyway, I set to work cutting the rope around my wrists. I cut myself many times, but finally I did it. I took down the Faust and Mephistopheles picture and waited by the door. This time I wasn't going to give up! Well, eventually I heard the key turn in the lock. Conrad came in followed by a man I knew as Number 14, whose head I brought the picture down on."

"Good lad!"

"I ran out through the door and felt a small hand thrust into mine. Annette locked the door, pointed to a ladder and told me to climb while Conrad banged on the door. In the dusty attic Annette told me to climb down when they went into the room and to pull a cord I would find behind a cupboard in the shadow of the staircase. I gave her the key and watched her climb down into the crowd that had gathered outside the room. As soon as she let them into the room I climbed down the ladder and hid behind the cupboard. I pulled the cord and heard a pile of pots fell over in the attic."

"What a brave young woman!"

"Well, of course they thought I had gone up the ladder, so that's where they went. I ran down the stairs and out into the road. I was free! I called for Annette, but I heard her voice cry out, 'This is a terrible house. I want to go back to Marguerite. To Marguerite. *To Marguerite!*'"

"You didn't go back for her?"

"I did. I ran up the stairs but Conrad ran straight into me. Well, he ran straight into my fist actually. He went down. But then a bullet grazed my neck, so I decided it was time to get out. I headed for Whitehall to find Carter."

"What an amazing story!"

"Thank you. At least one of the Young Adventurers has been busy. But there's more. I read a newspaper on my way to see Carter. There was an article on Kramenin, the man behind the revolution in Russia and who had just arrived in London as an unofficial on government business. I recognized his face. It's Number 1."

"Outstanding detective work, Mr. Beresford!"

"Thank you. But I still haven't finished. Carter was angry that I had come to his office, but when I told him everything that had happened he agreed that I was quite right to come and made a few telephone calls. Soon we were screaming around the streets of Soho in a police car. On the way I told him that the 29th was the important day. Carter said that he knew a General Strike had been planned for that day. He said the Government could deal with the strike, but if the top-secret papers were found, there would be trouble. Anyway, we didn't find anything in the house, except broken glass and pots. The gang had gone, so I came back to the Ritz."

Ritz Dining Room

# Chapter 18 — The Telegram

"Well, I think I have the answers to some of your questions Mr. Beresford," Julius said, over dessert. "First of all, I'd better tell you what adventures we've been having."

Julius told Tommy everything, focusing in particular on the part about Jane's loss of memory and Boris's visit to the apartment of Mrs. Vandemeyer.

"I'm not the only one who has been busy then!" Tommy declared, when the American had finished. "I can see how they guessed I knew nothing when I talked about questioning Jane. I couldn't have had any answers, because she couldn't remember!"

"Exactly!"

"But how did they know I was staying at the Ritz?"

"I don't know. Perhaps they just guessed. If your government covers all expenses for Carter's men, it would make sense."

"I hadn't thought of that. If we're finished eating, we can go and see if Tuppence had returned."

"Yes, let's do that."

Tuppence wasn't in her room, but while Julius checked his own room for any sign of her a small boy in a hotel suit spoke at Tommy's elbow:

"The young lady—she's gone away by train, I think, sir," he murmured shyly.

"What?" Tommy wheeled round upon him. The small boy became pinker than before.

"The cab, sir. I heard her tell the driver Charing Cross and to look sharp."

"When?"

"About half-past twelve. Just after I gave her a telegram, sir."

"Julius!" Tommy cried. "She's gone to Charing Cross station!"

Julius locked his door and joined Tommy, holding a note in his hand.

"She left you a note?" Tommy asked.

"It's nothing. Private."

"Private? Nothing about where she's gone?"

"I'm afraid not."

"Tell me in a cab. We have to hurry!"

"Yes."

The small boy still stood beside Tommy, who reached into his pocket and handed over thirty cents.

"One thing more," Tommy asked the boy. "What did she do with the telegram?"

"She threw it in the fireplace, sir, saying something like 'Whoop!'"

Tommy dug the telegram out of the fire ashes and read it to Julius:

> Come at once, Moat House,
> Ebury, Yorkshire, great develop-
> ments—Tommy.

They looked at each other, confused. Julius spoke first:

"You didn't send it?"

"No!"

"Then they've got her! They signed your name and took her!"

"Oh, Tuppence! Come on!"

On the train Julius explained that he had offered to marry Tuppence and handed over the note, which Tommy read to himself:

> Dear Julius,
> It's always better to have things in
> black and white. I don't feel I can
> be bothered to think of marriage

until Tommy is found. Let's leave
it till then. Yours affectionately,
Tuppence.

Tommy felt happy that Tuppence had
thought of him first, but also disappointed
that she seemed willing to accept Julius's
offer.

"Of course, I have heard that all women
refuse at least once. It's their way!" Julius
said suddenly.

"Refused?"

"Of course. Didn't I tell you she refused
me?"

"Oh Tuppence!" Tommy thought, "How
wonderful you are."

Moat House was empty when they finally reached the windswept village in
Yorkshire. They stayed in the Yorkshire
Arms and made frequent visits to the house
but had nearly given up when Tommy
picked up a gold brooch on the driveway.

"That's Tuppence's!"

They felt sure that Tuppence had at least
been there at some time, but after a week
they had found no further trace of her.

"A week until the 29<sup>th</sup>!" Tommy said. "They'll have no need for a hostage then, and her life won't be worth anything!"

"Yes! Damn it! I'm getting the police. We should have done it in the first place. We're no good as detectives, and it's a lady's life that's at stake here. You stay here and keep a lookout."

But Tommy received a telegram at the Yorkshire Arms later that day:

Join me Manchester Midland Hotel. Important news. Julius.

Julius met Tommy on Manchester station platform.

"You found her?" Tommy asked.

"No, but Peel Edgerton telegrammed me to say he had found Jane Finn and would be here."

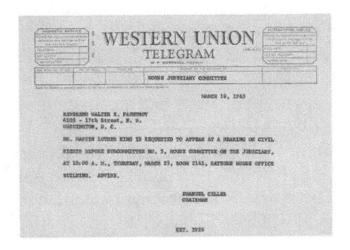

# Chapter 19 — Jane Finn

Julius introduced Sir James Peel Edgerton to Tommy in the hotel restaurant. Quickly, Julius started asking where Jane was and whether he could see her.

"That's not possible. She's been knocked over by a car and is recovering in hospital. But she gave her name as Jane Finn. That's a sign that she has recovered her memory."

"Ah! The doctor said a shock might do the trick!" Julius replied. "Is she badly hurt?"

"Just a scratch or two. But she's been asleep ever since."

"After the meal, I will go and see her," Julius said.

"Impossible!" Sir James said. "Visiting hours are over for tonight. Tomorrow would be fine. Ten o'clock."

"Very well! If you insist!" Julius replied, looking angry.

"I am told you have had an adventure of your own, Mr. Beresford."

Tommy told Sir James of his adventure in the Soho house. Sir James seemed particularly curious about what Annette had shouted when he escaped.

"No doubt she wanted to be back with Rita—Mrs. Vandermeyer."

"Yes, I suppose so. It's a shame such a pretty girl is in with crooks."

"And what have you been doing since?"

"Trying to find Tuppence of course!"

Sir James seemed shocked. He stared at Tommy with eyes opened slightly wider than usual.

"You mean Julius didn't tell you about the telegram?" Tommy added.

After Tommy had told Sir James everything about their search, the lawyer replied:

"They're holding her as a hostage, in case you talk."

"Yes, I worked that out," Tommy said.

"But she's safe, as long as they don't know we have Jane Finn. I guess you know how they must have found out about Tuppence?"

"No. Actually, I don't."

"Mr. Brown."

"I don't believe in Mr. Brown!" Julius said.

"No, you don't. But he exists, alright."

The three men arrived at Jane Finn's ward within the hospital at 10 o'clock sharp.

"Miss Finn," Sir James said. "This is your cousin, Julius P. Hersheimmer."

The girl, white bandages wrapped around her head, blushed and took Julius's hand.

"Are you really Uncle Hiram's son?" she asked.

"Sure am!"

"They've been telling me terrible things; that I lost my memory and that it is now five years after the sinking of the Lusitania!"

"There was a man aboard the boat," Sir James began. "He had important papers. Did he give them to you?"

"Yes. But I don't have them. I hid them inside a cliff outside Hollyhead."

"What?"

"People were following me. I didn't know what else to do."

"Describe the place," Tommy said.

"There's a path that leads down to the cliff and then down to the beach past big, yellow gorse bushes. On the path there is a rock that looks just like a begging dog at head height, and behind it a crevice, just bigger than my hand. I put the packet in there and shoved in some gorse twigs to cover it."

Tommy stood up to leave, but Sir James told Jane to finish the story.

"After that I took a train, but this woman in my carriage—a very beautiful, elegant woman—nodded to a man and something hard hit me on the back of my head. I don't remember anything more after that."

"Rita!" Sir James said.

Julius took Jane's hand.

"Jane, lie here and rest. We're going to get that packet right now!"

# Chapter 20 — Too Late

There's not much to tell about the hunt for the packet, except to say that Julius and Tommy found it, right where Jane said it would be. When they opened it, however, they found only a blank sheet of paper, which read:

HA! HA!
MR. BROWN

"No time to waste!" Tommy cried. "The game's up! We have to warn Carter as soon as possible."

"I've failed!" Tommy told Carter, in his office.

"Ah! Don't take it personally lad. You were up against the best. I blame myself. Especially since the other news."

"What other news? Tuppence?"

"Read for yourself."

Tommy read the report in front of Carter.

Body washed up on Yorkshire coast.

Description of Clothing: Green hat, coat with handkerchief in pocket marked A.D.F.

"I'm so sorry," Carter said.

Holyhead

## Chapter 21 — Tommy Makes A Discovery

Tommy returned to the Ritz hotel, feeling desperately sad, but a fire had started to burn, deep inside him. He wanted revenge.

"I'll find that Mr. Brown and make sure he hurts nobody ever again!" he told himself.

"They are saying something terrible about Tuppence!" Julius cried, rushing in.

"What do you care? It's all just money to you."

"You're probably right, son. But in any case, I'm off to Yorkshire. I want to see for myself before I'll believe it."

"Do what you like."

Tommy sulked in his room for a while and then picked up the single letter that lay on his table, a letter of consolation from Sir James.

"Better answer it I suppose."

But he had no paper, so he went to Julius's room to find some. He opened a drawer and almost fell on the floor.

"What's a photograph of Jane Finn doing in Julius's drawer?"

## Chapter 22 — In Downing Street

The British Prime Minister turned to Carter and said:

"Do you really things aren't so desperate after all?"

"Tommy Beresford doesn't seem to think so."

He handed over a letter.

> Dear Mr. Carter,
> I don't think Tuppence is dead—I have no doubt that body is not hers—and I don't think the girl in hospital is the real Jane Finn. I finally worked out who Mr. Brown really is and where the packet must be. I have sent a separate letter to you with all the details, but don't open it until midnight on the 28th. If you do, you will endanger not only me but Tuppence too. Also, please send the telegram on the second page to the Ritz.
> Tommy

At that moment the door opened and in walked Sir James Peel Edgerton.

"Sir James," Carter said. "Did you know Tommy is off on another attempt to catch Mr. Brown?"

"Yes. I wrote to him and he wrote back. He also told me something I didn't know before. He found a photograph of the French girl, Annette, in Julius's drawer."

"Well, what could that mean?" the Prime Minister asked.

"It means," Carter said, "that Annette is probably the original Jane Finn and that the photograph never left Julius in the first place."

"You mean … ."

"Yes, sir. It looks likely that the American is a fake and that this Jane Finn was on their side all along. In fact, I think Julius could be Mr. Brown."

"Incredible! And what is this telegram we're supposed to send?"

Carter cleared his throat and recalled it out loud:

Come at once, Astley Priors, Gatehouse, Kent. Great developments. Tommy.

"You see," Sir James said, "Julius and Tommy were in such a hurry go follow Tuppence that they assumed the boy in the hotel misheard Charing Cross for King's

Cross. But in fact, Mr. Brown had changed the original telegram—just a few words—to send them to Moat House in Yorkshire instead. We got hold of a copy of the original telegram, and it says Astley Priors. Astley Priors belongs to a Dr. Adams. And the best station to get there *is* Charing Cross"

"Well, what are you waiting for!" the Prime Minister said. "Get down there! That boy needs help!"

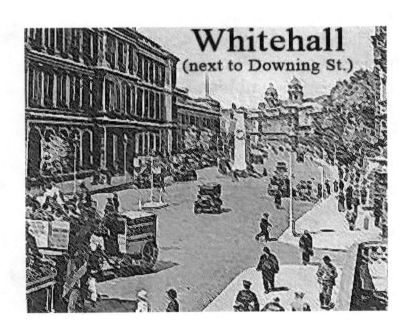

# Chapter 23 — A Race Against Time

Two days later Julius returned and found a note from Tommy that said he had gone to Argentina and wouldn't be back.

"Damned fool!" the American cried.

Astley Priory was a pleasant, red-brick building surrounded by woodland, which sheltered it from curious eyes on the road. Tommy had found out from asking around in the village that the nursing home catered for patients with 'diseases of the mind.' But by the second day, the 27th, he still hadn't found out any more.

Then he had a stroke of luck. He happened to walking into the village when, coming up behind him, a woman asked him the time.

"I have to get back in a hurry!" she explained.

"You work in the big house then?"

"Astley Priory. I have a lot of patients to cook for."

"Hm." Tommy thought quickly. "I suppose it's just English patients."

"Mostly, but we have one French girl."

"Oh, I see."

"Here's the shop. Good bye."

Tommy could hardly contain his excitement. He made his mind up to watch the house all night if necessary. Peering out from behind a tree he was rewarded when someone on the second floor stepped in front of a light, showing their shadow on the blind.

"I'd know that shadow anywhere!" Tommy told himself. "Tuppence."

Risking everything, Tommy couldn't help sneaking up to the house until he was beneath the window and whistled a tune he and Tuppence loved. Suddenly the front door opened. Two men chased Tommy down the driveway and back toward the village, but he reached the hotel before they saw where he went. Two hours later Tommy sneaked back to the tree in the grounds of the house and found a piece of paper, wrapped around a stone, on the lawn

"A note from Tuppence!"

It said: Tomorrow—same time.

## Chapter 24 — Julius Takes A Hand

Kramenin, the Russian diplomat, had just finished work for the day when the door to his office flew open.

"Hands up!" cried Julius, pointing his revolver.

"What have I done? Do you want money?"

"No, I want Jane Finn."

"Jane who? I don't know a Jane Finn!"

"Liar! You have five seconds to tell me where she is. After that, there will be a neat hole through your head."

"You wouldn't dare."

"Oh yes, I would!"

"I can't."

"Afraid of Mr. Brown?"

"Yes."

"You have a chance with Brown. You have no chance with this." Julius cocked the gun.

"Alright! Alright! She's at Astley Priors, Gatehouse, Kent!"

"Good! Come on! We haven't much time."

"What do you mean? I'm not coming!"

"Yes, you are."

Julius told his driver to put his foot on it and the Rolls Royce reached Astley Priors within an hour.

"Ring the bell and keep the engine running, George!" Julius told his driver.

Julius prodded Kremenin to the front door with the barrel of his pistol. The terrified Russian had already been told what to say:

"Bring down the girl, at once!"

"Why?"

"The game's up! Scotland Yard will be here in a few minutes. We have to take the girl as a hostage. Orders from *him*."

"Right!"

One minute later Whittington shoved the girl into the car and ran back to fetch his own things. Julius yelled:

"Drive!"

The Rolls Royce skidded out of the driveway and shot down the road with a roar.

"Get on the floor!" Julius yelled, as a bullet smashed through the rear window.

More bullets followed, but eventually they could only hear the sound of the car's engine.

"Where's Tommy?" Tuppence asked, putting her head up.

"In Argentina! Damned fool!"

"But he can't be!"

But Kremenin interrupted her by crying out:

"Let me go! If you let me go now, I have a chance!"

Julius made George slow the car and pushed the Russian out of the door, but before the car accelerated again, Tommy climbed in.

"Tommy!" Tuppence cried, hugging him.

"I saw the whole thing. I only just managed to grab the rear mudguard of the car. It was hell to hold on! Julius, you're a hero!"

"We're just coming to a crossroads!" George called out. "I had to get away fast, so I don't know where we are!"

"Annette!" Tommy cried, seeing the face of the other girl. "But I guess I should call you Jane?"

"Yes, I'm Jane Finn," the beautiful girl replied, in an American accent.

"Jane!" Julius cried.

"Who are you?" Jane asked.

"Your cousin, Julius Hersheimmer."

"Stop the car!" Tommy yelled. "There's a station just around the corner and a train in 3 minutes. You two ladies need to be on it!"

# Chapter 25 — Jane's Story

They had only travelled half the distance to London when Jane asked:

"You've been looking out of the window for nearly ten minutes. What are you thinking about?"

"Something. Something I think Tommy has guessed as well. I think we're still in great danger Jane. Anyone could be with Mr. Smith."

They reached London safely and Tuppence shook Jane gently awake.

"I didn't think we would make it this far!" Jane said.

"It will be more dangerous from now on."

Tuppence led Jane to a cab, but when it stopped at the first set of traffic lights, she opened the door and dragged Jane into a cab going in the other direction.

"That will throw them off our trail if they're following!" Tuppence said.

Tuppence still watched carefully through the window, so she saw the accident coming. Another cab slammed into theirs, pushing it onto the sidewalk.

Tuppence opened the door and led Jane down a narrow road.

"We're not far now!" she cried.

"Where are we going?"

"Sir James. We'll be safe there."

Tuppence glanced behind her at three men following on foot. She increased her speed, but by the time they entered Carlton House Terrace, the men were only a few paces behind. A large man stepped in front of them and blocked their path.

"Step aside!" Tuppence cried.

"I just want a word with—"

Tuppence head-butted him, a tactic she had once used at school. The man sat down on the pavement, winded and surprised.

Tuppence reached Sir James's door and banged on it, out of breath.

"What's going on?" he said, opening it.

The men in the street suddenly faded away.

"We've been chased," Tuppence gasped. "This is Jane Finn."

Sir James gave them both a stiff brandy and set them down in front of the fire, which had been lit.

"There is something I haven't told *any-one*!" Jane suddenly cried, standing up.

"Now's the time!" Sir James said, "if it will help us find the packet."

"It will. After being rescued from the sinking Lusitania, we docked at Holyhead. I escaped from the crowd of survivors and hid the packet beneath a cliff—"

"We know all this!" Sir James said, impatiently.

"Oh. But did you know that I had already substituted the document with two sheets of blank writing paper on the train?"

"No!" Sir James said, sitting down.

"There were many people watching me. I had to be careful, so I took the document out of the packet and put it between two pages of a magazine I had bought. I stuck those pages together with gum from a couple of envelopes and put the magazine in my coat pocket. Then I resealed the packet with the blank paper inside. After somebody hit me over the head, they took me to a house in Soho—"

"Tommy told us all about it," Tuppence said.

"Well, when they found out the document had gone, they said they would torture me if I didn't tell them where I had hidden it. I didn't know what to do.

Suddenly, I had a bright idea. I started
speaking in French and pretended I had lost
my memory. Of course, at first, they didn't
believe it, but a man called Whittington
said I couldn't be that clever, and he ordered a woman who had befriended me on
the ship called Mrs. Vandermeyer to look
after me."

"What happened to the packet?" Sir
James asked.

"They kept me in a room without a window, but luckily they hadn't bothered to
look inside the magazine. Late that first
night I carefully unsealed the two pages
and hid the document in the paper backing
of a picture on the wall, a Faust; Marguerite with her box of jewels."

"Yes! Apart from a trip to Bournemouth
when Mrs. Vandemeyer sought a cure for
my imaginary illness, I spent the whole
time there, until Tommy arrived."

"It's still there then!" Sir James cried,
standing up.

"That's why you went back into the
house crying out something about Marguerite!" Tuppence said. "It was a message for
Tommy!"

# Chapter 26 — Mr. Brown

Sir James was already putting on his coat.

"To Soho at once!" he cried.

"Wait!" Tuppence cried. "There is something you need to know. The identity of the real Mr. Brown."

"I already know it Miss Cowley. Julius Hersheimmer is Mr. Brown."

Both women gasped.

"Who else could have poisoned Mrs. Vandermeyer that night?"

The police guards around the Soho house knew Sir James well, so they let him straight through. He didn't take long to put his penknife to the backing of the Faust picture and produce the ill-fated document.

"At last!" he cried.

"I sense danger!" Tuppence whispered. "We must get out of here fast."

"Yes, you sense danger," Sir James echoed. "You sense the presence of Mr. Brown."

"But how could he have got in?" Tuppence asked, looking around her.

"Don't you understand?" Sir James said, pulling out a revolver and pointing it at Tuppence. "*I* am Mr. Brown!"

Both women gasped, but suddenly a familiar American drawl said:

"Caught you red-handed!"

Julius Hersheimmer seized the man with the gun from behind in an iron grip.

Quick as a flash the prisoner's hand bearing a large signet ring flew to his mouth. With a shudder he fell forward in a crumpled heap, leaving the faint smell of bitter almonds hanging in the air.

# Chapter 27 — A Supper Party at the Savoy

The 29th, Labour Day, passed with nothing more eventful than a few marches in Hyde Park, but the Government knew it had had a close shave. Newspapers announced the untimely death of Sir James Peel Edgerton, but it didn't mention that he had been killed by cyanide, putting his death down to heart-attack, so his reputation and that of the lawyer class was saved.

On the 30th, Julius took Tuppence aside in the Ritz and handed her a blank cheque.

"I want a party tonight for Jane that nobody will ever forget. Spare no expense!"

"Alright. But you haven't asked for my answer yet."

Julius sweated while Tuppence kept him in suspense.

"Well?" he finally prompted.

"Oh, you idiot. I knew you were never interested in me. You love Jane! I consider that you have rejected me, rather than the other way around."

Both of them laughed until their ribcages ached.

When Jane finally took her place at the head of the banqueting table, the crowd of guests drew in their breath. Her hair seemed more flecked with gold than ever, and the gold shone more brightly, all over the most beautiful dress anybody had seen that year.

Tommy stared at her wide-eyed.

"Do you have any regrets?" Tuppence whispered to him.

"None. You did a wonderful job with her."

"Ha! I didn't really have to try. But I do love you Tommy."

"I know. I love you too. That's the important thing. The Young Adventurers will have more adventures, and we will become very rich!"

"I'll drink to that!"

"I just found out that you all suspected me!" Julius told them, when the meal had finished. "But you were all wrong about something."

Even the Prime Minister leaned in close to hear his answer.

"I did lose the photograph in fact. I found it again inside Mrs. Vandemeyer's safe."

"Ah! I thought you found something," Tuppence replied.

"She's a first-class detective," Carter said, proudly.

# Chapter 28 — And After

Two cars sped across Hyde park after the party. In one sat Julius and Jane.

"Jane, you are saved now but still have no family."

"Yes, it's true. I would dearly love somebody to take care of me. But I simply cannot think who!"

Jane had a wicked twinkle in her eye that made Julius laugh.

"How about a millionaire like me? I've loved you since the moment I saw you."

"Oh Julius! Do you really mean it?"

"Yes."

"Then I accept!"

The couple embraced and kissed for the first time, before Julius whispered to the chauffeur:

"Take the long way around the park. Shall we say, about three hours?"

In the second car, Tuppence and Tommy sat at either ends of the rear seat. For some reason that neither could fathom, they felt farther apart since solving the case.

"Are you going to marry him?" Tommy suddenly said suddenly.

"Julius? I forgot that you knew. Well, he has a lot of money."

"Oh, women are impossible!"

"Did you know we're both going to get a big cheque for solving the crime."

"Hm." Tommy sulked while he looked out of the window.

"I love detective work," Tuppence said. "It's almost as good as shopping."

"What for?" Tommy said, only half paying attention.

"Oh, things for a house; furniture, bright carpets and a bed with lots of cushions. Possibly a house, perhaps a flat."

"Whose house?"

"You think I don't want to say it, but I don't mind. Ours!"

"Oh, you darling!" Tommy said, putting his arms around her.

# Biography of Lazlo Ferran

Educated near Oxford, during English author Lazlo Ferran's extraordinary life, he has been an aeronautical engineering student, dispatch rider, graphic designer, full-time busker, guitarist and singer, recording two albums. Having grown up in rural Buckinghamshire Lazlo says:

"The beautiful Chiltern Hills offered the ideal playground for a child's mind, in contrast to the ultra-strict education system of Bucks."

After a long and successful career within the science industry, Lazlo Ferran left to concentrate on writing.